Galactic Ganja Guide

Galactic Ganja Guide

Matthew Petchinsky

Apophis Enterprises LLC

1

<u>Galactic Ganja Guide</u>
<u>By:Matthew Petchinsky</u>

-

-

-

<u>Preface</u>

Welcome to a journey that transcends the boundaries of space, time, and consciousness. "Galactic Ganja Guide" is an exploratory odyssey that marries the ancient Earth-born tradition of cannabis cultivation and usage with the boundless possibilities of interstellar travel. This guide serves not just as a manual to the multifaceted world of cannabis but also as a passport to the cosmos, where we hypothesize its spread and evolution across galaxies, engaging with civilizations and cultures as diverse and complex as the universe itself.

Cannabis, with its deep roots in the history of Earth, has been a companion to humanity for thousands of years, serving medicinal, recreational, and spiritual purposes. Its significance is not merely confined to its psychoactive properties but extends to its role in culture, medicine, and even the economy. As we embark on this speculative venture into the galaxy, we imagine how this resilient and versatile plant might have traversed the cosmic winds, finding its way to alien worlds and becoming an integral part of extraterrestrial societies.

The hypothetical spread of cannabis throughout the galaxy serves as a fascinating lens through which we can explore the concept of panspermia - the theory that life exists throughout the Universe, distributed by space dust, meteoroids, asteroids, comets, planetoids, or potentially by spacecraft in the form of unintended contamination by microorganisms. Through this prism, we envision cannabis seeds journeying across the cosmos, taking root in distant worlds, each with its unique environment, thereby giving rise to an astonishing variety of cannabis-like substances. These substances, with their myriad effects, uses, and cultural significances, provide a rich tapestry of alien flora that mirrors the diversity of life itself.

Understanding the relationships diverse alien cultures have with these cannabis-like substances opens a window into their societies, beliefs, and values. Just as cannabis has played a myriad of roles in human history –

from sacred rituals to the center of contemporary legal and ethical debates – its extraterrestrial counterparts could serve as focal points of cultural practices, religious ceremonies, or even as catalysts for intergalactic diplomacy and conflict.

In this guide, we delve into these speculative narratives with a spirit of curiosity and openness, drawing on the rich tapestry of human experiences with cannabis as a foundation. We explore not just the science of cannabis and its potential interstellar variations but also the cultural, spiritual, and sociopolitical dimensions of its use across the universe. From the terrains of Earth to the outer edges of the galaxy, "Galactic Ganja Guide" invites you on an unprecedented adventure that challenges the imagination, expands the mind, and unites the cosmos through the shared language of cannabis and its cosmic kin.

As we traverse this uncharted galaxy of green, let us keep in mind the importance of respect, understanding, and the responsible exploration of these substances. The journey through "Galactic Ganja Guide" is as much about exploring the outer reaches of space as it is about understanding the inner space of consciousness and the universal connections that bind us all. Welcome aboard, cosmic traveler, to an adventure like no other.

Chapter 1: The Botany of Cannabis in the Cosmos

An Interstellar Journey through Cannabis Botany

The journey of understanding cannabis in the cosmos begins with a foundational overview of its botany. On Earth, Cannabis sativa, Cannabis indica, and Cannabis ruderalis have adapted to diverse climates, demonstrating the plant's remarkable versatility. These species undergo a well-documented life cycle from seed to sprout, to vegetative growth, flowering, and finally, to seed production, closing the circle of life. Beyond the terrestrial, when we cast our gaze to the stars, we delve into the realm of speculative evolution—how this resilient plant might adapt and thrive in the myriad environments of distant worlds.

Cannabis strains on Earth have been selectively bred for various traits, including THC and CBD content, resistance to pests, and climatic adaptability. Genetic manipulation has pushed this further, tailoring strains to specific medical conditions and recreational effects. Transposing this concept to interstellar scales, we might imagine genetic engineers crafting strains for growth in low-light conditions of distant planets orbiting dim stars, or strains that thrive in the thinner soils of asteroid-based habitats.

Speculative Evolution Across the Galaxy

As we imagine cannabis taking root in alien soils, its evolutionary journey likely diverges in fascinating ways, driven by the unique conditions of each world. On planets with denser atmospheres, plants might develop thicker stalks and broader leaves to support their weight and maximize light absorption. In contrast, worlds with lower gravity could see the emergence of taller, more delicate structures, reaching skyward with ease.

Adaptation might also extend to the plant's psychoactive properties. For example, in environments rich in certain minerals or exposed to unique forms of radiation, we could speculate the development of new cannabinoids with effects unknown to human science. These alien compounds could offer unexplored medicinal benefits or novel psychoactive experiences, broadening the horizons of both science and recreation.

The Science of Astro-Botany

Astro-botany, the study of plant life in space, offers insights into how cannabis and other plants might be cultivated in off-Earth environments. In zero-gravity conditions aboard space stations, plants face unique challenges, including the absence of traditional "up" and "down," affecting how roots and shoots grow. Water and nutrients distribution also behaves differently in microgravity, requiring innovative hydroponic systems for plant sustenance.

Research has shown that with the right support systems, plants can indeed grow in space, adapting to the lack of gravity. For cannabis, this implies the potential for cultivation aboard spacecraft and space habitats, using specialized growth chambers. These chambers would regulate factors like light, water, nutrients, and atmosphere composition, simulating the plant's natural conditions as closely as possible. Such technology not only allows for the production of cannabis in space for medicinal and recreational use but also serves as a model for growing a variety of crops, supporting long-term human habitation beyond Earth.

Towards a Galactic Green Thumb

In imagining the botany of cannabis across the cosmos, we stand at the confluence of science and speculation, drawing on what we know to explore what might be. From the genetic manipulation of strains to thrive in extraterrestrial environments, to the speculative evolution of cannabis on worlds far from our own, and the pioneering science of astro-botany, we begin to sketch a vision of a galaxy where cannabis joins humanity in its journey among the stars.

This exploration is not merely academic; it represents a bridge between our earthly experience and the vast potential of the cosmos. As we extend our reach into the galaxy, cultivating cannabis and other crops in space, we take with us a piece of our home, weaving the familiar into the fabric of the unknown. In doing so, we carry forward the spirit of discovery and adaptability that has long defined our species, planting seeds—both literal and metaphorical—for future generations to cultivate.

If you want to see some amazing products, please visit my Virtual Dispensary: https://shift.store/sg1fan23477/retail

Chapter 2: The Intergalactic Cannabis Archive

A Cosmic Compendium of Cannabis

The Intergalactic Cannabis Archive serves as the galaxy's most comprehensive catalog of cannabis strains, documenting the botanical treasures that span across star systems. This living document is not merely a collection of data; it represents a confluence of science, culture, and the art of cultivation that stretches from the verdant fields of Earth to the terraformed landscapes of distant exoplanets. Each entry in the archive details a strain's genetic heritage, psychoactive properties, and the unique adaptations that allow it to thrive in its native cosmic environment.

The Alchemy of Genetic Engineering

In the age of interstellar exploration, genetic engineering has emerged as a cornerstone technology, enabling botanists and geneticists to design cannabis strains with unprecedented precision. This scientific prowess has given rise to strains with unique properties tailored to a wide array of uses—from medical treatments targeting specific alien pathogens to recreational varieties offering experiences unimaginable with Earth-origin strains.

One of the most remarkable advancements has been the development of strains designed for extreme environments, such as the high-radiation zones of neutron star proximities or the low-light worlds of distant solar systems. These strains exhibit novel photosynthetic pathways and radiation-resistant DNA, showcasing the ingenuity of genetic manipulation.

Industrial uses have also seen significant innovation, with strains engineered for biofabrication purposes. These varieties produce fibers and bio-plastics with extraordinary tensile strength and flexibility, suited for constructing habitats in harsh extraterrestrial conditions. This functional diversification of cannabis underscores the plant's integral role in the sustainability and expansion of human presence in the galaxy.

Cultural Significance Across Civilizations

As humanity ventured beyond its solar cradle, it encountered myriad alien cultures, each with their unique relationships to cannabis and its extraterrestrial analogs. For some, these plants hold sacred significance, woven into the fabric of spiritual practices and ceremonies. In such societies, specific strains have been cultivated for millennia, their effects honed to induce states of consciousness conducive to communion with the divine or the universe itself.

In other cultures, cannabis-like substances serve as the cornerstone of social interactions and diplomacy. Rare and highly prized strains act as gestures of goodwill among interstellar neighbors, facilitating bonds across the stars. These cultural exchanges have enriched the Intergalactic Cannabis Archive, transforming it into a mosaic of galactic biodiversity and interspecies friendship.

The archive also details the role of cannabis in the arts and sciences of various civilizations. From enhancing creativity and cognitive flexibility to serving as a subject of scientific inquiry into the nature of consciousness and biochemistry, cannabis and its cosmic variants have deeply influenced the intellectual and artistic landscapes of numerous societies.

The Living Legacy of the Intergalactic Cannabis Archive

The Intergalactic Cannabis Archive is more than a repository of information; it is a testament to the adaptability and enduring allure of cannabis throughout the galaxy. It symbolizes a shared journey of discovery, unity, and the ceaseless pursuit of knowledge across the cosmos. As we continue to explore the uncharted reaches of space, the archive grows, enriched by each new strain and story it encompasses, weaving an ever-expanding tapestry of cosmic biodiversity.

This chapter has only begun to unveil the complexity and diversity of the galactic cannabis experience. As the archive evolves, it invites us to ponder not just the biological and chemical intricacies of these plants but also the deeper connections they foster among the myriad forms of life that gaze upon the stars and dream of what lies beyond.

If you want to see some amazing products, please visit my Virtual Dispensary: https://shift.store/sg1fan23477/retail

Chapter 3: Cultivation Techniques Across the Stars

Earthly Foundations and Cosmic Cultivation

The art and science of cannabis cultivation have deep roots on Earth, honed over millennia through traditional agricultural practices and modern technological innovations. These terrestrial techniques have laid the groundwork for the cosmic cultivation methods that now allow humanity and other space-faring civilizations to grow cannabis under the stars. This chapter delves into the comparative analysis of cultivation on Earth and its expansion into the cosmos, exploring the integration of advanced technologies and the creative adaptation required for interstellar agriculture.

Terrestrial Techniques: A Baseline for Innovation

On Earth, cannabis cultivation ranges from the sun-drenched fields of outdoor farms to the controlled environments of indoor grow operations. These methods leverage the planet's natural resources—soil, water, and sunlight—while also employing techniques like hydroponics, aeroponics, and artificial lighting to optimize growth and potency. Soil-based grows, for instance, benefit from the complex ecosystem services provided by microorganisms, whereas hydroponic systems allow for precise control over nutrients and water, leading to higher yields in smaller spaces.

Cosmic Cultivation: Adapting to New Worlds

The transition from Earth's hospitable climes to the harsh environments of other planets and space habitats necessitates a radical rethinking of cultivation techniques. In space habitats and orbiting stations, gravity—or the lack thereof—presents unique challenges for water and nutrient delivery, necessitating closed-loop hydroponic or aeroponic systems with artificial gravity or centrifugal force to simulate terrestrial conditions. Lighting, too, must be carefully managed with LED arrays that mimic the spectrum of sunlight, critical for photosynthesis and plant development.

Terraformed worlds offer a different set of challenges and opportunities. Here, the creation of a viable ecosystem for cannabis cultivation involves not only adjusting the soil composition and atmospheric conditions but also introducing microorganisms and pollinators to recreate the complex interdependencies found in Earth's biosphere. These efforts are augmented by advanced genetic engineering techniques, creating strains specifically adapted to the peculiarities of each terraformed environment.

The Frontier of Hybridization and Genetic Engineering

At the forefront of extraterrestrial cannabis cultivation is the art and science of hybridization and genetic engineering. These disciplines merge traditional breeding practices with cutting-edge biotechnology to produce strains capable of thriving under extraterrestrial conditions. Geneticists focus on traits such as radiation resistance, low-light photosynthesis, and efficient nutrient uptake to ensure that these plants can withstand the extremes of space travel and alien environments.

This effort goes beyond mere survival, aiming to preserve the diverse array of cannabinoids and terpenes that define cannabis's medicinal and recreational properties. Through meticulous selection and breeding, cultivators can enhance these traits, ensuring that even in the most distant colonies, the essence of cannabis remains true to its earthly origins while embracing the unique characteristics of its new celestial homes.

Conclusion: The Harmonization of Art and Science

The cultivation of cannabis across the stars represents a harmonious blend of art and science, tradition, and innovation. It reflects humanity's enduring relationship with this plant, carrying it with us as we reach for the stars. As we continue to explore and settle new worlds, the techniques and technologies developed for cosmic cultivation will not only advance our ability to grow cannabis but also deepen our understanding of life's potential in the cosmos.

The knowledge gained from these interstellar agricultural endeavors enriches the collective heritage of all space-faring civilizations, marking our shared journey through the galaxy. As we cultivate cannabis among the stars, we also sow the seeds of future discoveries, ensuring that as we grow outward into the universe, we also grow inward, cultivating a deeper connection with the natural world and with each other.

If you want to see some amazing products, please visit my Virtual Dispensary: https://shift.store/sg1fan23477/retail

Chapter 4: Galactic Ganja Cuisine

Culinary Cosmos: An Introduction to Intergalactic Edibles

Galactic Ganja Cuisine explores the art of creating edibles and beverages infused with cannabis and its alien counterparts, diving into a universe where culinary innovation meets ancient tradition. This chapter serves as a guide through the diverse culinary landscapes of the galaxy, showcasing recipes that blend the psychoactive elements of cannabis with the flavors and traditions of various worlds. It highlights the cultural significance and etiquette of sharing these potent meals, offering a taste of the communal and spiritual experiences that transcend planetary boundaries.

Recipes from the Stars: Cannabis-Infused Delicacies

The culinary application of cannabis and similar substances in galactic cuisine is as varied as the cultures that dot the cosmos. On some planets, traditional dishes may include a mild infusion of cannabinoids to enhance flavor and induce a sense of well-being, while others might favor stronger concoctions for their psychoactive effects.

- **Terraformed Terra Cotta Tea**: A popular beverage brewed with a blend of Earth's finest cannabis leaves and the nectar of Zephyr flowers from New Mars. This tea is renowned for its calming effects and its ability to enhance interplanetary communication skills.

- **Quantum Quiche**: A dish that combines genetically modified fungi from Europa, with a dash of powdered cannabis sativa, resulting in a meal that bends the perception of time, popular among time travelers and historians alike.

- **Stellar Soma Salad**: A vibrant, raw salad made with a mix of leafy greens from Terra Nova, tossed in a dressing infused with a mild psychoactive extract derived from the indigenous Xyank weed. This salad is known for stimulating creativity and is a staple among artists and creators.

Culinary Traditions Across Planets

Beyond individual recipes, cannabis and its interstellar variants play significant roles in the culinary traditions of many planets. For instance, on the water world of Aquarius Prime, meals begin with a ceremonial ingestion of a cannabis-like aquatic plant extract, believed to align diners with the planet's natural rhythms. In contrast, the desert planet of Sandara celebrates the end of their solar cycle with a feast featuring dishes infused with a potent desert bloom that shares similarities with Earth's cannabis, marking a time of renewal and reflection.

Each planet's unique ecosystem contributes to the diversity of ingredients available for culinary exploration, leading to a rich tapestry of flavors and effects. These traditions are not just about sustenance but are deeply interwoven with the cultural and spiritual life of the inhabitants, offering insights into their values, history, and relationship with the natural world.

Etiquette and Cultural Significance

The act of sharing ganja-infused meals goes beyond mere consumption; it is a gesture of friendship, respect, and communal bond. In many societies, such meals are accompanied by rituals and ceremonies that underscore their importance. For example, before partaking in a communal meal on the forest moon of Sylvan, participants often share stories of gratitude, acknowledging the plants, the planet, and each other.

This shared experience is seen as a pathway to understanding and peace among diverse cultures. The etiquette surrounding these meals emphasizes mindfulness, respect for the plant and its effects, and an appreciation for the company of fellow diners. It is a time when differences are set aside, and commonalities are celebrated, fostering a sense of unity and interconnectedness.

Conclusion: A Universe of Flavors

Galactic Ganja Cuisine offers a glimpse into the vast possibilities of culinary exploration and cultural exchange in the galaxy. Through the shared language of food and the psychoactive experiences provided by cannabis and its cosmic cousins, we find a universal thread of connection. These dishes and traditions invite us to expand our palates, minds, and spirits, exploring the rich diversity of the cosmos one bite, sip, and shared meal at a time.

If you want to see some amazing products, please visit my Virtual Dispensary: https://shift.store/sg1fan23477/retail

Chapter 5: Medicinal Uses Throughout the Milky Way

Healing Herbs of the Cosmos

The exploration of the Milky Way has not only expanded humanity's geographical knowledge but has also dramatically broadened our medicinal horizons. This chapter delves into the diverse ways in which various civilizations across the galaxy utilize cannabis and analogous plants for healing, highlighting the role of alien cannabinoids in treating diseases unknown to Earth and examining how ethnobotanical studies integrate extraterrestrial plant medicine into human healthcare systems.

The Universal Pharmacy: A Spectrum of Healing

Across the galaxy, the therapeutic applications of cannabis and its cosmic cousins vary as widely as the planets they inhabit. Earth's understanding of cannabis as a medicinal plant—used to treat conditions ranging from chronic pain to epilepsy—serves as a mere starting point. As we encounter new civilizations, we discover plants with similar properties but adapted to different ecosystems, offering a broader spectrum of cannabinoids and other active compounds.

- **Regenerative Resin from Regulus IV**: On this forested world, the native species use a cannabis-like resin that accelerates cellular regeneration, making it invaluable in treating injuries and promoting recovery from surgery. Human researchers are studying its potential applications in regenerative medicine and anti-aging treatments.
- **Nebula Nectar on Nimbus-9**: The inhabitants of Nimbus-9 have developed a nectar derived from their local variant of cannabis, effective in treating a wide range of neurological conditions. This nectar has shown promise in alleviating symptoms of neurodegenerative diseases, offering hope for conditions previously deemed untreatable.

Alien Cannabinoids and Unknown Diseases

The introduction of alien cannabinoids into the pharmacopeia offers groundbreaking treatments for diseases that have long plagued humanity, as well as newly encountered conditions arising from interstellar travel and colonization. The unique biochemical structures of these compounds interact with the human body in novel ways, offering therapeutic effects beyond the reach of Earth-origin medicines.

For instance, a cannabinoid complex identified in the Andromedan plant Xyphoria has been found to neutralize a class of pathogens resistant to all known antibiotics, providing a powerful new tool in the fight against infectious diseases. Similarly, the psychoactive properties of certain extraterrestrial plants have been utilized to treat mental health conditions, offering new pathways to psychological well-being.

Ethnobotanical Integration: Bridging Worlds

The integration of extraterrestrial plant medicine into human healthcare represents a fascinating field of ethnobotanical study, bridging cultural and biological knowledge across the stars. This integration involves not only the scientific analysis of plant properties but also an understanding of the cultural contexts in which these plants are used for healing.

Collaborative research with alien civilizations allows for a respectful exchange of knowledge, ensuring that the medicinal uses of these plants are understood and appreciated in their full complexity. This approach not only enriches human medicine but also fosters a deeper connection and mutual respect among the diverse cultures of the galaxy.

Future Horizons in Galactic Medicine

As we continue to explore the Milky Way, the potential for discovering new medicinal plants and compounds seems limitless. The medicinal uses of cannabis and similar substances throughout the galaxy underscore the importance of preserving planetary ecosystems and respecting the knowledge of all civilizations we encounter.

This ongoing journey promises not only advancements in healthcare but also a deeper appreciation for the interconnectedness of life across the cosmos. Through the lens of medicinal botany, we see a future where healing transcends planetary boundaries, and the welfare of all beings is enhanced by the shared bounty of the galaxy's flora.

If you want to see some amazing products, please visit my Virtual Dispensary: https://shift.store/sg1fan23477/retail

Chapter 6: Recreational and Ritualistic Uses

An Intergalactic Cultural Tapestry

The journey through the cosmos reveals a rich tapestry of cultures, each with its unique relationship to cannabis and similar substances. These relationships, spanning recreational enjoyment to profound spiritual and ritualistic practices, showcase the diverse ways in which beings across the galaxy celebrate, commune, and connect with the universe and each other. This chapter explores the myriad recreational and spiritual uses of cannabis across different civilizations, offering a comparative analysis of their social functions and ceremonial significance.

Recreational Revelations: A Spectrum of Joy

Recreational use of cannabis and analogous substances serves as a universal language of joy, relaxation, and creativity among many galactic societies. On Earth, the social and recreational use of cannabis is well-documented, from casual gatherings to artistic and musical inspiration. Similarly, across the galaxy, beings have harnessed the euphoric and mind-expanding properties of these plants to enhance sensory experiences, social interactions, and the appreciation of art and nature.

- **The Festivals of Fornax**: On Fornax, a planet known for its vibrant social life, the annual Bloom Festivals celebrate the harvest of their native psychoactive flora. These festivals are characterized by elaborate light shows, music performances, and communal consumption of various edibles and inhalants, fostering a sense of unity and collective joy.
- **Zero-G Zest on Zenith Station**: Aboard Zenith Station, orbiting a neutron star, the microgravity environment adds a unique twist to cannabis consumption. Here, "smoke orbs" filled with vaporized cannabinoids float freely, with inhabitants enjoying the chase and capture of these orbs as part of the recreational experience.

Rituals and Reverence: Connecting with the Cosmos

Beyond recreation, many cultures imbue cannabis and its counterparts with deep spiritual significance, incorporating them into rituals that connect individuals to the divine, the universe, or their deeper selves. These practices often emphasize the sacredness of the substance, its role in facilitating transcendental experiences, or its capacity to symbolize or effect spiritual transformation.

- **The Circle of Cynosure**: On the oceanic world of Cynosure, the aquatic beings use a cannabis-like seaweed in their Moon Tide Ceremonies to achieve a deep, empathetic connection with their planet's vast oceans. Consumed in a ritualistic setting, it allows participants to experience the ebb and flow of tides within their own consciousness, deepening their bond with the natural world.

- **Spectral Spirits on Spectra**: The ethereal inhabitants of Spectra engage in a ceremony known as "Veil Viewing" using a crystalline substance with properties akin to THC. This ceremony is believed to thin the veil between dimensions, allowing participants to communicate with ancestral spirits and gain wisdom from beyond the physical realm.

The Impact of Interstellar Trade

The interstellar trade of cannabis and similar substances has significantly impacted the availability and diversity of recreational and ritualistic materials. Trade routes crisscrossing the galaxy enable the exchange of not just goods, but cultural practices and spiritual traditions, enriching the social and spiritual lives of many civilizations.

This cosmopolitan exchange has led to the fusion of recreational and ritualistic practices, with beings adopting and adapting the customs of distant worlds, creating a shared galactic heritage. However, this exchange also raises questions about preservation, commodification, and respect for the sacredness of these practices and substances.

Conclusion: A Galactic Mosaic of Meaning

The recreational and ritualistic uses of cannabis and its galactic counterparts paint a picture of a universe united by common threads of joy, community, and spiritual search. These practices, varying widely across cultures, highlight the profound ways in which beings seek connection—to each other, to nature, and to the cosmos. As we navigate the vast expanse of the galaxy, understanding and respecting these diverse expressions of life and consciousness become crucial to our shared journey through the stars.

If you want to see some amazing products, please visit my Virtual Dispensary: https://shift.store/sg1fan23477/retail

Chapter 7: Law, Trade, and Ethics in the Galactic Cannabis Economy

Legal Labyrinths: Navigating Planetary Jurisdictions

The legal landscape governing cannabis and its cosmic counterparts is as varied and complex as the galaxy itself. Across different planetary jurisdictions, the status of these substances ranges from fully legal and regulated markets to strict prohibition. This diversity reflects the myriad cultural, spiritual, and social values attached to psychoactive plants and their derivatives. Some worlds embrace these substances for their medicinal and spiritual benefits, integrating them seamlessly into society. Others, citing concerns over health, social order, or moral values, impose stringent controls or outright bans.

- **The Confederacy of Aligned Systems** has established a galaxy-wide framework for the regulation of psychoactive substances, including cannabis, allowing for medical and religious use while imposing strict guidelines on recreational consumption.
- **On Terra Nova**, a planet with a rich history of botanical medicine, cannabis and similar substances are fully legal, celebrated for their healing and spiritual properties, and integrated into daily life.
- **The Zentari Collective**, however, has banned all psychoactive substances, including cannabis, due to a cultural emphasis on mental discipline and purity.

Interstellar Trade Agreements: The Tangle of Transgalactic Trade

The trade of cannabis and analogous substances between star systems introduces a complex web of legal and logistical challenges. Interstellar trade agreements must navigate the disparate laws of participating worlds, creating a framework that respects planetary sovereignty while facilitating commerce. These agreements often include clauses on the standardization of product quality, safety regulations, and the prevention of smuggling and illegal trade.

The Galactic Trade Consortium, for example, has established a certification system for psychoactive botanicals, ensuring that only products meeting rigorous safety and ethical standards are traded. This system aims to protect consumers, respect the laws of member planets, and prevent the exploitation of less developed worlds.

Ethical Considerations: A Galactic Conscience

In a galaxy where cannabis and similar substances are as diverse as the cultures that use them, ethical considerations in cultivation, distribution, and consumption take on paramount importance. Issues such as the environmental impact of cultivation, the rights and welfare of workers, and the potential for abuse and addiction require thoughtful examination and action.

- **Sustainable Cultivation**: As demand for cannabis and similar substances grows, so does the need for sustainable cultivation practices that minimize environmental impact. This includes the use of renewable energy sources, water conservation techniques, and organic farming practices that preserve planetary ecosystems.
- **Fair Trade Practices**: Ensuring that the benefits of the galactic cannabis economy reach all participants equitably is a significant ethical concern. Fair trade initiatives focus on supporting small-scale farmers and workers, ensuring fair wages, safe working conditions, and community development.
- **Responsible Consumption**: With the diversity of psychoactive substances available across the galaxy, educating consumers about the effects, proper dosages, and potential risks is essential for promoting responsible use. Public health campaigns and access to reliable information play a critical role in preventing abuse and ensuring the well-being of individuals and communities.

Conclusion: Forging a Future of Responsible Stewardship

As humanity and other space-faring civilizations navigate the complexities of the galactic cannabis economy, the path forward requires a balance of legal acumen, ethical integrity, and mutual respect. By addressing the legal, trade, and ethical challenges with a commitment to sustainability, equity, and health, the galaxy can cultivate a cannabis economy that benefits all beings. This chapter underscores the importance of collective responsibility and cooperation in shaping a future where the cultivation, distribution, and consumption of cannabis and its cosmic counterparts reflect our highest values and aspirations.

If you want to see some amazing products, please visit my Virtual Dispensary: https://shift.store/sg1fan23477/retail

Chapter 8: Cannabis and Consciousness Expansion

The Galactic Mind: An Introduction to Cosmic Consciousness

In the vast expanse of the galaxy, consciousness exploration stands as a unifying quest among myriad beings. Cannabis and its interstellar analogs play a pivotal role in this journey, serving as keys to unlocking realms of awareness beyond the ordinary. This chapter delves into the theories and practices surrounding cannabis and consciousness expansion, exploring how various alien races harness these substances for interdimensional awareness, communication, and spiritual connection with the cosmos.

Diverse Pathways to Expanded Awareness

Across the galaxy, civilizations have developed unique approaches to consciousness exploration using psychoactive substances. These methodologies reflect the rich tapestry of galactic culture, philosophy, and spirituality.

- **The Echoing Meditation of Eridani**: On the water-covered planet of Eridani, the aquatic inhabitants use a cannabis-like seaweed in their Echoing Meditation, a practice that enables them to experience the collective memories of their ancestors, stored in the planet's vast oceanic consciousness.
- **Spectral Shifts on Sigma-7**: The avian species of Sigma-7 consume a crystalline substance with properties similar to THC to facilitate "Spectral Shifts," a state of heightened perception that allows them to see beyond the visible spectrum and communicate with the energy beings residing in their dimension.
- **The Dream Weavers of Drax**: Utilizing a potent vapor derived from their native psychoactive flora, the Dream Weavers of Drax induce shared dream states that are believed to offer insights into the fabric of reality, weaving consciousness with the cosmic tapestry.

Interdimensional Awareness and Communication

The role of psychoactive substances in achieving interdimensional awareness and communication is a profound area of study among galactic scholars. These experiences often defy conventional understanding, suggesting that consciousness may operate across dimensions beyond physical space-time.

- **Intergalactic Channeling Circles**: Some cultures hold intergalactic channeling circles, where participants consume cannabis-like substances to synchronize their vibrations with those of distant civilizations, facilitating telepathic communication and the exchange of knowledge.
- **The Portal Gardens of Persephone**: On Persephone, elaborate gardens serve as interdimensional portals. Here, ingesting specific combinations of psychoactive plants, including cannabis analogs, prepares the mind to navigate these portals, exploring new dimensions of existence and consciousness.

Comparative Spirituality: Connecting with the Cosmos
The spiritual use of cannabis and its equivalents in connecting with the cosmos reveals a shared curiosity and reverence for the mysteries of existence. This comparative spirituality highlights the universal quest for understanding, belonging, and transcendence.

- **The Cosmic Web Rituals**: Practiced by several space-faring cultures, these rituals involve the use of cannabis-like substances to perceive and interact with the Cosmic Web, the interstellar network of energy that binds the galaxy. Participants describe experiencing a profound sense of unity and interconnectedness with all life.
- **Harmonization Ceremonies on Harmonia**: The Harmonians use a unique blend of psychoactive herbs, including a cannabis variant, in their Harmonization Ceremonies to align their individual consciousness with the harmonic frequencies of the universe, fostering peace, insight, and cosmic coherence.

Conclusion: The Universal Quest for Expanded Consciousness

The exploration of consciousness through cannabis and similar substances represents a universal quest that transcends planetary boundaries. This journey into the depths of the mind and the vastness of the cosmos underscores a shared desire among beings of the galaxy to understand the nature of reality, connect with the divine, and expand the horizons of awareness. Through these diverse practices and experiences, the galaxy's inhabitants continue to explore the infinite possibilities of consciousness, fostering a deeper understanding and unity among the stars.

If you want to see some amazing products, please visit my Virtual Dispensary: https://shift.store/sg1fan23477/retail

Chapter 9: The Future of Galactic Ganja

Visionary Horizons: Cannabis in Cosmic Evolution

As we stand on the cusp of a new era in interstellar society, cannabis and its galactic counterparts continue to weave their threads into the fabric of cosmic civilization. This chapter embarks on a speculative journey into the future of Galactic Ganja, exploring advancements in research, its potential as a peace-making tool among civilizations, and the quest for the ultimate strain that could unite the galaxy in harmony.

Frontiers of Research: Beyond the Known

The future of cannabis research holds promise for breakthroughs that could redefine our understanding of biology, consciousness, and the very essence of interstellar coexistence. With the advent of quantum botany, researchers are beginning to unlock the subatomic properties of cannabis, revealing how its compounds interact with the quantum field of consciousness. This burgeoning field suggests that cannabis may play a crucial role in facilitating quantum entanglement between minds, enabling a form of communication and empathy previously unimaginable.

- **Synthetic Cannabinoid Creation**: Innovations in synthetic biology might allow scientists to design cannabinoids in the lab, tailoring their effects to target specific medical conditions or enhance cognitive and sensory experiences without any side effects.
- **Cannabis as a Cosmic Connector**: Research into the electromagnetic properties of cannabis and its analogs suggests these plants might act as natural antennae, capable of tuning into cosmic frequencies that promote interstellar communication and understanding.

Cannabis: A Catalyst for Galactic Peace

In a galaxy brimming with diverse civilizations, each with its unique perspectives and potential for conflict, cannabis emerges as a potent tool for fostering peace and understanding. Through shared experiences of consciousness expansion and the breaking down of barriers that psychoactive substances can facilitate, erstwhile adversaries might find common ground.

- **Diplomatic Rituals**: Future interstellar diplomacy could see the adoption of cannabis-infused ceremonies, where leaders partake in ritualistic consumption to enhance empathy, dissolve prejudices, and negotiate with open hearts and minds.
- **Intercultural Exchanges**: Cannabis and its variants could drive intercultural exchange programs, promoting peace through understanding by allowing beings from different worlds to experience each other's perspectives and traditions in a profound and transformative way.

The Quest for the Ultimate Strain

The ultimate dream of Galactic Ganja enthusiasts and researchers alike is the creation or discovery of the ultimate strain—a strain that not only embodies the pinnacle of therapeutic and recreational potential but also possesses the unique ability to unite diverse galactic civilizations in harmony. This mythical strain, often referred to as "The Harmonizer," is said to adapt to the user's individual physiology and consciousness, providing exactly what is needed for healing, enlightenment, or bliss.

- **Universal Adaptability**: "The Harmonizer" would possess a chameleonic quality, changing its effects based on the user's species, biology, and current state of mind, making it universally beneficial.
- **Empathogenic Properties**: Beyond mere recreation or therapy, this strain would enhance empathetic connections, enabling users to deeply understand and feel compassion for other beings, regardless of their origins.

Conclusion: A Green Galaxy Awaits

As we gaze into the future, the potential of Galactic Ganja to transform interstellar society is boundless. From groundbreaking research that pushes the boundaries of science to its role in fostering peace and under-standing among civilizations, cannabis and its cosmic variants stand as beacons of hope and unity. The ongoing quest for "The Harmonizer" epitomizes the aspirational spirit of the galaxy's diverse inhabitants—a shared dream of harmony and connection. In the vast expanse of space, amidst the stars and nebulae, the future of Galactic Ganja unfolds as a testament to the power of exploration, innovation, and the universal quest for peace.

If you want to see some amazing products, please visit my Virtual Dispensary: https://shift.store/sg1fan23477/retail

Epilogue: The Cosmic Cannabis Connection

As we conclude our journey through the "Galactic Ganja Guide," we find ourselves at the nexus of space and consciousness, having traversed the vast expanse of the galaxy to explore the myriad ways in which cannabis and its interstellar analogs weave through the fabric of cosmic society. This voyage has illuminated not just the diversity of applications and cultural significances of cannabis across the stars but also underscored the universal aspects of the cannabis experience—a testament to its power to connect, heal, and expand horizons.

Reflections on a Galactic Journey

Our expedition has revealed cannabis as a multifaceted gem of the cosmos, serving as a medicine, a sacrament, a source of inspiration, and a catalyst for peace and understanding. Through the lens of galactic ganja, we have glimpsed the potential futures of humanity and our interstellar neighbors, where the ancient plant continues to play a pivotal role in society, spirituality, and science.

This journey has also highlighted the adaptability of cannabis, evolving across worlds and ecosystems to meet the needs of countless beings. Its ability to foster connections—between individuals, between cultures, and even between dimensions—speaks to a profound truth about the universe: at the heart of existence is a desire for unity and understanding.

The Symbolic Significance of Cannabis

Cannabis emerges from our explorations as a bridge—a botanical bridge that spans galaxies, cultures, and consciousness itself. Its presence in so many worlds and its capacity to harmonize so many aspects of life underscore its symbolic significance as a connector, a healer, and a teacher. In every leaf, bud, and crystal, there lies a microcosm of the galaxy's vastness and variety, a reminder of the common threads that bind us all in the great cosmic tapestry.

This symbolic bridge invites us to cross from the known to the unknown, from the mundane to the miraculous, guiding our steps as we navigate the complexities of existence with curiosity, compassion, and an open mind. It encourages us to see beyond our differences, recognizing the unity in diversity as we share in the ancient, sacred ritual of cannabis consumption.

A Call to Responsible Exploration

As we stand at the threshold of new discoveries and new connections, "The Cosmic Cannabis Connection" serves as a call to responsible exploration. This exploration is twofold: it is an outward journey into the uncharted territories of space, where we seek to understand and respect the myriad forms of life and consciousness that populate the universe. Simultaneously, it is an inward journey into the depths of our own consciousness, where we use the insights gained from cannabis and its cosmic counterparts to deepen our self-awareness, expand our empathy, and cultivate a sense of interconnectedness with all beings.

The responsible exploration of outer space and inner consciousness through the lens of galactic ganja requires us to approach with humility, reverence, and a commitment to ethical engagement. It challenges us to consider the impact of our actions on other worlds and cultures, to engage in fair and sustainable practices, and to use the knowledge and experiences gained for the betterment of all.

In Conclusion: Toward a United Cosmos

"The Cosmic Cannabis Connection" beckons us toward a future where the galaxy is united not only through trade, diplomacy, and interstellar travel but through a shared appreciation for the profound and universal experiences that cannabis and its interstellar analogs facilitate. In this future, cannabis stands as a symbol of peace, understanding, and the endless potential for growth and connection.

As we close this guide, let us carry forward the lessons and insights it has offered, cherishing the cosmic cannabis connection as a precious gift—a key to unlocking the doors of perception, bridging worlds, and fostering a galaxy-wide community bound by mutual respect, curiosity, and love. In the leaf, the bud, and the boundless stars, we find our kinship, our hope, and our destiny.

Further Reading and Resources for the Galactic Ganja Guide

The exploration of cannabis in a galactic context opens up vast territories of knowledge, spanning botany, anthropology, pharmacology, and beyond. For those eager to delve deeper into the themes presented in the "Galactic Ganja Guide," this list of further reading and resources offers a gateway to a more profound understanding and appreciation of cannabis and its cosmic journey. These resources are designed to enrich your exploration, providing insights into the science, culture, and spiritual aspects of cannabis and similar substances across the galaxy.

Books and Publications

- **"Cosmic Botany: A Guide to Extraterrestrial Plant Life"** by Dr. Xenia Flora - An expansive look at the flora of the galaxy, with a chapter dedicated to psychoactive plants, including those similar to cannabis.

- **"Interstellar Pharmacopeia: A Comprehensive Guide to Space-Faring Botanicals"** edited by Prof. Liora Quasar - This comprehensive guide explores the medicinal and therapeutic uses of plants found throughout the galaxy, offering detailed insights into their biochemistry and applications.

- **"The Ethnobotany of the Cosmos"** by Dr. Soren Leafsong - Focusing on the cultural and spiritual significance of plants, including cannabis, across different civilizations, this book offers an anthropological perspective on plant use in ritual and society.

- **"Quantum Consciousness and the Eighth Dimension"** by Dr. Hal Cyon - A speculative exploration into the role of psychoactive substances in accessing higher dimensions of consciousness, with theoretical foundations and anecdotal evidence.

Journals and Periodicals

- **Galactic Botanical Review** - A peer-reviewed journal offering the latest research on extraterrestrial plant life, including studies on psychoactive plants and their effects on various species.

- **Interstellar Anthropologist Quarterly** - Features articles on the cultural practices of alien societies, with special issues dedicated to the use of psychoactive substances in rituals and social settings.
- **Quantum Mind & Consciousness** - A publication that delves into the intersection of consciousness studies and quantum mechanics, exploring how substances like cannabis can affect perceptions of reality.

Online Resources and Communities

- **GalactiFlora Database** - An online database of plants discovered across the galaxy, including user-generated content on cultivation tips, effects, and medicinal uses.
- **The Cosmic Connection Forum** - A vibrant online community of explorers, researchers, and enthusiasts discussing their experiences with galactic ganja and other psychoactive substances.
- **SpaceFarer's Guide to Galactic Botany** - An online course offering comprehensive lessons on the cultivation, use, and cultural significance of extraterrestrial plants, including cannabis analogs.

Virtual Reality Experiences

- **"Journey Through the Cosmic Garden" VR Experience** - An immersive virtual reality tour of planets known for their unique flora, providing an up-close look at the cultivation and use of cannabis-like plants in various ecosystems.
- **"Mindscapes: An Intergalactic Psychedelic Adventure"** - A VR simulation that allows users to experience the consciousness-expanding effects of alien psychoactive substances in a safe and controlled environment.

Workshops and Conferences

- **Galactic Botany Symposium** - An annual event that brings together scientists, researchers, and enthusiasts to share discoveries, cultivation techniques, and cultural insights related to extraterrestrial plant life.
- **Consciousness Across the Cosmos Workshop Series** - Workshops focusing on the role of psychoactive plants in expanding consciousness, featuring speakers from diverse scientific and spiritual backgrounds.

Conclusion

The resources provided here are intended to spark curiosity, expand knowledge, and encourage a respectful and mindful approach to the exploration of cannabis and its cosmic counterparts. Whether through the pages of a book, the community of an online forum, or the immersive experience of virtual reality, there is a universe of knowledge waiting to be discovered. Let the "Galactic Ganja Guide" be your starting point on a journey of cosmic proportions.

-

-

-

<u>Message from the Author:</u>

I hope you enjoyed this book, I love astrology and knew there was not a book such as this out on the shelf. I love metaphysical items as well. Please check out my other books:

-Life of Government Benefits

-My life of Hell

-My life with Hydrocephalus

-Red Sky

-World Domination:Woman's rule

-World Domination:Woman's Rule 2: The War

-Life and Banishment of Apophis: book 1

-The Kidney Friendly Diet

-The Ultimate Hemp Cookbook

-Creating a Dispensary(legally)

-Cleanliness throughout life: the importance of showering from childhood to adulthood.

-Strong Roots: The Risks of Overcoddling children

-Hemp Horoscopes: Cosmic Insights and Earthly Healing

- Celestial Hemp Navigating the Zodiac: Through the Green Cosmos

-Astrological Hemp: Aligning The Stars with Earth's Ancient Herb

-The Astrological Guide to Hemp: Stars, Signs, and Sacred Leaves

-Green Growth: Innovative Marketing Strategies for your Hemp Products and Dispensary

-Cosmic Cannabis

-Astrological Munchies

-Henry The Hemp

-Zodiacal Roots: The Astrological Soul Of Hemp

- **Green Constellations: Intersection of Hemp and Zodiac**

-Hemp in The Houses: An astrological Adventure Through The Cannabis Galaxy

Check out my Virtual dispensary for all your hemp needs: https://shift.store/sg1fan23477/retail

If you want solar for your home go here: https://www.harborsolar.live/apophisenterprises/

Instagrams: @apophis_enterprises, @hempkingdom2024, @apophisbookemporium, @apophisfashion, @apophisscardshop

Twitter: @apophisenterpr1, Tiktok:@apophisenterprise

Youtube: @sg1fan23477

Podcast: Apophis Chat Zone: https://open.spotify.com/show/5zXbrCLEV2xzCp8ybrfHsk?si=fb4d4fdbdce44dec

Newsletter: https://apophiss-newsletter-27c897.beehiiv.com/